Tiny

essentials of
donor loyalty

White Lion
Press

Tiny

essentials of
donor loyalty

by Adrian Sargeant

Published by
The White Lion Press Limited
567 Ben Jonson House
The Barbican
London
EC2Y 8NH

© 2010 Adrian Sargeant/The White Lion Press
ISBN 13: 978-0-9553993-3-6
ISBN 10: 0-9553993-3-5

First printed 2010

Cover photography by Ken Burnett
Other photography by Ken Burnett, Rozenn
Hamoniau

Design and print production by em associates

Printed and bound by CPI Group (UK) Ltd,
Croydon, CR0 4YY

Contents

The author

Adrian Sargeant is the Robert F Hartsook Professor
of Fundraising at Indiana University. He is also
Professor of Nonprofit Marketing and Fundraising
at Bristol Business School (UK) and an Adjunct
Professor of Fundraising at the Australian Centre
for Philanthropy and Nonprofit Studies,
Queensland University of Technology, Brisbane,
Australia. He is one of the world's foremost
authorities in the domain of nonprofit marketing
and fundraising. He is the managing editor of the
*International Journal of Nonprofit and Voluntary
Sector Marketing* and the author of *Fundraising
Management* and *Building Donor Loyalty*, published
by Routledge and Jossey Bass, respectively.

Preface

You don't earn loyalty in a day.
You earn loyalty day-by-day.

Jeffrey Gitomer, USA
businessman, author
and public speaker

Loyalty, as we use the term, means faithful adherence to our cause. Resolute, committed, unfailing. People talk of loyalty as fierce: descriptions of loyal people are usually prefaced by words like devoted, steadfast and unshakable.

So donor loyalty is not likely to be easily acquired. It has to be earned. But once earned, it endures. Loyalty, therefore, is likely to be hugely valuable and universally valued. If your professional commitment is to the donor-centred approach to raising money that is known as relationship fundraising then, for you, donor loyalty is your El Dorado.

No one in the world knows more about this elusive essence than Professor Adrian Sargeant. He doesn't just talk about donors and donor loyalty and he doesn't just rely on anecdotes from those donors that he has read about or met. His observations are underpinned by detailed research. In a specialist subject that boasts few experts

Adrian Sargeant has studied loyalty professionally, academically, practically and in depth, earning him a reputation that places him at the pinnacle of his field.

Adrian's edge is that he has a unique mastery of the subject. Now he presents his findings – just the key issues, just the essentials, just what really matters for fundraisers. This Tiny book is a distillation of all that donor development professionals need to have to hand if they are to understand and get close enough to their donors to stimulate, nurture and build real, durable loyalty.

In just 10 short chapters – *why bother?, satisfaction, encouraging dissent, commitment, trust, identity and identification, what damages loyalty, recruiting loyal donors, other issues and conclusions* – Adrian Sargeant effectively sets out the blueprint for understanding, overcoming and capitalising upon what he describes in his very first sentence as, '...the single biggest challenge facing our sector today.'

He's not wrong. But now you can respond effectively and comprehensively to this challenge, just by spending an hour or so with this packed, but tiny, easy-to-use book

Why bother?

Building donor loyalty is the single biggest challenge facing our sector today. Despite increasing interest, nonprofits both large and small continue to lose their donors at an astonishing rate. Not many businesses would survive if they lost a third of their customers in the course of the year, yet this is a statistic that is commonplace in our sector. To make matters worse, this figure refers only to our friends, people that have given at least two donations to a favoured charity. When you look at newly recruited supporters the figure is actually a good deal worse. Only around half, or fewer, of the individuals who at one point can be motivated to send us a cheque will ever give to us again.

So, does this matter? After all, many organisations have existed for years and seem to have coped admirably with this pattern of performance. Services are still provided for our beneficiaries and organisations continue to survive. That being the case, why bother with loyalty? If it's such a big deal why hasn't there been more interest in actively trying to build loyalty to date?

Good question, particularly when the implications of these appalling rates of retention are so profound. Even small improvements in donor loyalty can have a huge impact on the returns an organisation is able to generate from its fundraising. In other words, we are wasting potentially enormous sums of money by failing to address the issue.

To illustrate, over the years I have been involved with the analysis of many different nonprofit databases and have been able to model the impact of different levels of donor loyalty on the future value of an organisation's relationships with its donors. Typically a 10 per cent improvement in the level of loyalty now increases the lifetime value of the fundraising database by around 50 per cent. Yes, 50 per cent. This happens because the effect compounds over time. If you have 10 per cent more donors still giving at the end of the current year you have 10 per cent more people giving to the organisation through year two. In the second year you'll lose 10 per cent fewer of these and lose fewer of the balance in each subsequent year. Over time the effect mounts up. Begin to look out over a five-year horizon and small improvements in loyalty achieved now can deliver real fundraising value tomorrow.

Impressive though this may be it is certainly not the end of the story. Most organisations in our sector have to engage in significant donor recruitment activity. They have to find a multitude of new friends each year just to make up for all the individuals who are going to terminate their support. Unfortunately this activity costs money, a lot of money.

Most charities make a loss on their new donor recruitment activity. It isn't at all uncommon for charities to get back only half of the monies that they invest in attracting new donors. A new donor might cost, for example, £50 to £60, while her donation will be a fraction of that. The exact costs vary by charity and by the media that are being employed, but the implication is clear. If a charity is losing 10 per cent fewer of its donors each year, it doesn't have to continue to invest large sums of money in replacing them. Factor in these savings in 'acquisition' costs to our earlier considerations and my 10 per cent improvement in donor loyalty now can enhance the lifetime value of the fundraising database by as much as 100 per cent.

Most charities make a loss on their new donor recruitment.

Even this though isn't the end of the story. If donors stay around for longer they can often be persuaded to increase the level of their giving, move up from occasional to regular support, buy from the trading catalogue, volunteer time to a local group, donate clothes to a charity shop, recommend that friends offer their support and ultimately, perhaps, to consider offering a legacy in their will. Putting a cash value on these benefits isn't easy, but on average, if you try, you'll find that my 10 per cent increase in loyalty can increase the lifetime value of the fundraising database by as much as 200 per cent.

Be aware of the figures

Sometimes I've stood up at sector conferences and events, quoted these figures and seen a few eyes in the audience glaze over at this point. Many folks remain unconvinced by the maths despite the overwhelming evidence in its support. In reality the exact percentages are unimportant. It doesn't matter whether on average a 10 per cent increase in loyalty leads to a 50 per cent, 100 per cent, or 150 per cent increase in lifetime value. The point is that organisations need to know in their *specific* case what a difference it would make. Smart organisations make sure that all their fundraisers are aware of these figures too so that they can allocate their budgets accordingly. They also make sure that every donor-facing member of staff (or volunteer) is aware of these numbers, so that the next time anyone is tempted to be short with a caller, or fails to make that little extra effort to provide a requested piece of information, he knows what an impact this could have on the future of his organisation. The sector as a whole needs to wake up and do likewise.

Charities also need to think seriously about remunerating their fundraisers for the improvements in loyalty they are able to deliver. If even small improvements in loyalty can deliver such impressive improvements in value they should be the focus of significant management attention.

Throwing money away

The majority of commercial marketing managers are now remunerated, at least in part, for their achievement against some kind of benchmark for loyalty. Sadly this is not yet the case in the nonprofit world and, year after year, the sector continues to report astoundingly high levels of attrition. We should all hang our heads in shame. We are quite literally throwing our money away, continually seeking to top up what has become a very leaky bucket. To make matters worse it isn't even our own money we are wasting. These are all funds that were donated by our well-meaning supporters last year.

Given the current environment, if we fail to take action the situation can only get worse. In both the UK and the USA the size of the donor pool is actually contracting. Around two to five per cent fewer individuals are presently engaging with the sector each year. New donor recruitment will become increasingly more difficult and thus more expensive as a consequence. The costs of our current poor level of performance are therefore set to escalate. Be in no doubt, loyalty is most definitely an issue and the single biggest issue that our sector currently faces, because of the huge potential to increase our well-being if we get it right.

So how can an organisation build loyalty? This will be the focus of subsequent chapters. We will examine each key driver of loyalty in turn and then look at a range of specific actions a nonprofit can take to build it.

Donor satisfaction

I've lost count of the number of fundraising conferences I've attended where one speaker or another confidently tells his audience, 'Our research shows that donors only want three things, namely ....' Interestingly, the three things seem to vary by presenter, but it certainly isn't uncommon to be told that giving donors choice, thanking them properly and treating them courteously is all that matters. It all sounds delightfully intuitive. Unfortunately it is also delightfully wrong and a good clue that the speaker in question hasn't the first clue about retention.

Yes, things like these do matter, but they matter because they are a symptom of an underlying issue and it is this underlying issue that should be the focus of our concern, *not* the symptoms in isolation. To paraphrase one of the great marketing thinkers, Theodore Levitt famously noted that, in the service context, people generally only know what they want when they don't get it. Asking people what they want is therefore stunningly unreliable. Organisations need to look at the whole approach to donor care rather than focusing on specific dimensions. Thanking donors appropriately does matter, for example, but it is just one component of the overall quality of service we provide to them as fundraisers.

This thinking isn't new and it certainly shouldn't be regarded as controversial. We seem to be forever playing catch-up in the fundraising profession with lessons learned many years before in the commercial sector. Corporates have known for over 30 years that the single biggest driver of customer loyalty is their satisfaction with the quality of service provided. This is why customer satisfaction surveys are now so ubiquitous. Managers are hungry for the data and want to use them to inform their strategy. As I noted earlier, many managers are now remunerated on the basis of the improvements they are able to deliver in retention.

Customer satisfaction surveys typically ask customers to report how satisfied they are with each aspect of the service in turn and then conclude with an 'overall how satisfied are you?' question at the end. It is this latter question that is generally the focus of most managerial interest and with good cause. To illustrate, customers are often asked to indicate the degree of their satisfaction on a five-point scale such as:

1. Very dissatisfied.

2. Dissatisfied.

3. No opinion/neutral.

4. Satisfied.

5. Very satisfied.

Donor satisfaction

The reason for the commercial interest is that corporates discovered a long time ago that there is a world of difference between customers who indicate they are very satisfied and those that indicate they are just satisfied. On average, across a whole range of different contexts, customers who say they are very satisfied are six times more likely to buy again than those who are merely satisfied[1]. In the context of fundraising the multiple isn't quite so high but research still tells us that donors who are very satisfied are twice as likely to be giving next year as those who are merely satisfied.

So why is this? Well, if you have ever ticked the 'satisfied' box you have probably ticked it for a reason. The service was OK, but not outstanding. There was something they didn't handle well, or perhaps something you were looking for that didn't materialise. Little wonder then that large numbers of people who tick this box decide to go elsewhere the next time they need to make a similar purchase. The same is true in fundraising.

Quality of service

Of course donors aren't usually purchasing something for themselves. More usually they are looking to deliver a benefit for a needy child, an earthquake victim, or to someone ill with a life-threatening disease. Unfortunately for most donors they have little way of being able to directly assess the quality of the work the charity undertakes, so they draw conclusions about this, in part, through their own experiences as donors. They have no option but to use the quality of the service they are exposed to personally as a surrogate.

The upshot here is that charities need to measure donor perceptions of the quality of service provided to them. In doing this it is necessary to develop a measure that is properly tailored to the organisation. It will need to reflect the existing pattern of communication, the content, style and tone of that communication, the different ways in which donors can interact with the organisation, the manner in which any issues or complaints may be dealt with and (in a membership context) perceptions of the package of benefits that may be offered.

Some examples of appropriate questions are provided opposite.

Please rate your level of satisfaction with each of the following aspects of the service that XXX provides you with as a donor, where 1 = very dissatisfied and 5 = very satisfied

	Very dissatisfied	2	3	4	Very satisfied
Informing me how my money is spent.	☐	☐	☐	☐	☐
Not asking for support too often.	☐	☐	☐	☐	☐
Offering me some choice in the communications I receive.	☐	☐	☐	☐	☐
Thanking me appropriately.	☐	☐	☐	☐	☐
Recognising the contribution I've made in the past.	☐	☐	☐	☐	☐
Demonstrating they care about my needs.	☐	☐	☐	☐	☐
Making it clear why my continued support is needed.	☐	☐	☐	☐	☐
Giving me opportunities to support XXX in other (non-financial) ways.	☐	☐	☐	☐	☐
Using an appropriate style/tone in their communications.	☐	☐	☐	☐	☐

It is then possible to calculate an overall satisfaction score by adding up the scores for each of the items, or perhaps by taking the average of the scores across the survey. Some organisations take a different approach and pose an additional question asking donors directly how satisfied they are with the service overall. My personal preference is for the former approach as donors usually have some difficulty thinking about how satisfied they are with 'fundraising'. It is a lot easier to think about what we mean by fundraising and thus each of the dimensions of that service in turn.

A lot of organisations will stop there and assume the job is done. After all, each dimension of the service has now been assessed which is surely all that is important. Unfortunately not; the scores for the individual items are interesting but they can't be used to inform a retention strategy, at least not in isolation. The temptation when you measure only perceptions is to strive to improve any aspect of the service that achieved a low ranking. This is nonsense.

Focusing attention

To begin to take decisions about how to improve, it is necessary to understand first how important each dimension is to the supporter base. Some aspects of the service can receive low ratings, but if they aren't important to the donor there may be no real need to improve. By contrast, if low ratings are received on dimensions that are important to the donor then the fundraising team can focus their attention and resources at fixing the issue. An identical scale can be employed to measure importance, modifying the five-point scale to range from 'very unimportant' to 'very important'.

Armed with this information the fundraiser might then plot each dimension in a matrix such as that presented in figure 1. Service dimensions in the top left quadrant that score highly on both satisfaction and importance can be kept as is. The prescription here is essentially to 'keep up the good work'. In cases where the service scores highly on satisfaction but low in terms of importance, the suggestion is that the organisation may be indulging in overkill. It is very good at doing things of little consequence. Equally, where satisfaction levels are low and importance scores high, the prescription would be to invest. Here the organisation is weak at providing aspects of the service that really matter to

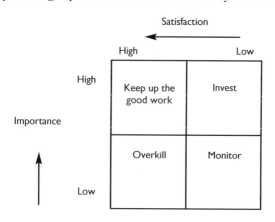

Figure 1: Importance/performance matrix

donors and these areas need to be improved. Finally, where satisfaction ratings are low and importance ratings are similarly low the prescription would be to 'monitor' these factors. These factors have a habit of becoming important over time so it is important to continue to check on them periodically.

There is a final layer of complexity in measuring donor satisfaction that fundraisers need to be aware of. To illustrate, imagine you've been invited out for dinner. Your partner gives the evening a big build up, telling you that the restaurant has had rave reviews, the food is stunning, the service first rate, the wine list extensive and the ambience attractive and relaxing. Unfortunately, when you arrive the experience turns out to be more on a par with what you might find in a mid-range hotel diner. You'd probably leave the restaurant pretty dissatisfied with the experience. Imagine though, that instead of the big build up, your partner had told you it was the only place he/she could book at short notice, that the menu is good, but somewhat limited in scope, that the service is functional and that the wine list is OK but unexceptional. In this scenario if you had an average kind of experience you might well leave the restaurant feeling at least satisfied with the evening.

What I'm trying to illustrate with this example is that donor satisfaction is not only a function of their perception of the experience, it is also a function of what they were expecting to receive from the outset. Of course, ask most donors what quality of service they were expecting to receive from the fundraising team and they will look at you with bewilderment. Many won't be able to conceptualise this in the abstract. It can therefore be more meaningful to use a proxy and see what donors experience from other charities they support. Whether they are consciously aware of it or not, how they are treated by other charities will certainly drive what they expect when they start giving to yours. In any case, it can be very helpful to have a sense of how one's own organisation compares against others in the sector, so this is a helpful proxy in all kinds of ways.

... new members will be expecting to enjoy a very specific set of promised benefits.

It is important to stress though that there *are* scenarios when it is perfectly meaningful to ask supporters what they were expecting. Some categories of supporters will have a clear view on this. In the membership context, for example, new members will be expecting to enjoy a very specific set of promised benefits. Asking about these benefits is entirely legitimate. It is therefore up to the organisation to select the best approach and to use a mirror of the scale we discussed earlier to capture the requisite data.

Thankfully it isn't necessary to approach every donor on the database for a view on these issues. A sample of each category of donor can be approached, perhaps on an annual basis, so that the organisation can track trends in the level of satisfaction over time. Smart organisations might want to combine this with market research on other issues, perhaps identifying ongoing donor needs and preferences and looking for feedback on ideas the fundraising team has for the future.

Maintaining a dialogue with supporters about these issues is key in fostering retention and offends no one. While organisations are sometimes reluctant to conduct this kind of research for fear of alienating donors, research tells us that folks like to be asked and will actually exhibit slightly higher levels of loyalty as a consequence. If you don't believe me, try monitoring the loyalty of donors you have posed questions to and compare this with the balance of the supporter base. I'll guarantee you will notice a marked increase in loyalty amongst those who participate in this way.

Encouraging dissent

This might sound rather counter-intuitive, but a further good way to build donor loyalty is to encourage dissent. Encouraging donors to complain when something goes wrong for them with the quality of service, where they disagree with the stance the organisation has taken on a specific issue, or with the decision to accept a particular corporate donation is actually a good strategy to adopt. This too is a piece of learning from the commercial sector. To illustrate, consider the graph in figure 2: here we are looking at the percentage of people who would buy again from a supplier under certain sets of circumstances. In the far left we have a group of people who have had a major problem with the service provided and who have chosen not to complain. In these circumstances only around nine per cent of these individuals would buy again if it was a major problem; 31 per cent if it was a minor problem. Moving slightly to the right we have a group of people who had a major problem and on this occasion they did complain. Unfortunately the organisation ignored them, but they did at least take the time to complain. In these circumstances around 18 per cent would buy again if it was a major problem, 46 per cent if it was a minor problem.

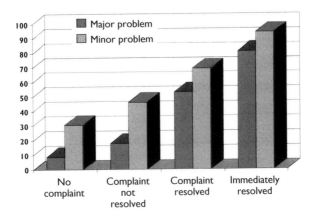

Figure 2: Percentage of customers who will buy again under certain circumstances

Shifting again to the right we have a group of people who had a major problem, complained and the organisation eventually put things right to their satisfaction, perhaps after a little effort and haggling on the part of the customer. Here 52 per cent would buy again if it was a major problem, 69 per cent if it was a minor problem.

Finally in the far right we have a group of people who had a major problem, they complained and the organisation was immediately able to remedy the situation to their satisfaction. In this scenario 81 per cent would buy again if it was a major problem, 94 per cent if it was a minor problem.

... it is no longer fashionable to talk about complaints. Today it is opportunities...

This tells us two very interesting things about human behaviour. Firstly, look at the difference between the groups who did not bother or who were not able to complain and the groups that complained and the organisation ignored them. Isn't this fascinating? Even organisations that genuinely don't give a damn about their supporters are still better off putting someone at the end of the phone to take the complaint. Individuals who get their complaints 'off their chest' are significantly more likely to give again than individuals who do not. This is why in America it is no longer fashionable to talk about complaints. Today it is 'opportunities', as in opportunities to build loyalty.

As though to emphasise this latter point, there is one crucial piece of information missing from this graph. In this fictitious example the average repurchase rate across people who never had a problem is 78 per cent. So now how do you build loyalty?

That's right, you go out and create thousands of problems for all your supporters and you very quickly put things right. The individuals exposed to this strategy will exhibit significantly higher levels of loyalty than those who never had a problem in the first place. Of course this is a high-risk approach and your trustees may not entirely approve! It does, however, reinforce the notion that complaints should be seen as opportunities.

... create mechanisms for donors to voice their concerns.

If you ever conduct this kind of analysis for your own organisation you will find that the percentages vary, but the relationship between the various boxes and the relationship between the boxes and the average loyalty rate will not. The pattern is one commonly exhibited across a whole range of different contexts.

As fundraisers we need to create appropriate mechanisms for donors to voice their concerns. In the UK, it is now a requirement that members of the Fund Raising Standards Board should have an appropriate complaints handling procedure in place. They must establish this before the organisation can join the scheme. This is to be applauded. It is not only good professional practice, it is also smart from the perspective of loyalty. I'd personally encourage complaints, not only about fundraising but about any aspect of the organisation's approach that the donor has an interest in.

Maximise the effect

Of course to maximise the effect it is important that each 'opportunity' is treated with respect and corrective action; an apology or an explanation of the organisation's approach should be provided within a reasonable period of time. The response should also respond to the specific points raised by the donor and not simply be, as is so often the case, a bland general acknowledgement of the donor's concern. All this latter approach indicates to the donor is that no one has an interest in what she thinks. To illustrate, over the years I've had cause to complain several times to various airlines and if I receive another standard letter from United telling me that it was 'good to hear what the experience felt like from my personal perspective' I think I'm liable to do someone an injury!

Before leaving this issue of opportunities, there is one further avenue that nonprofits should explore. Some individuals will stop giving and never bother to take the step of complaining when something goes wrong. It is important to know why people terminate their support so that any recurring themes can be tackled by the organisation. Exit polling of a sample of lapsed supporters is therefore a good practice to adopt. Many donors will stop giving because of a change in their financial circumstances and there isn't much a charity can do to influence that, but many donors will stop because of something the organisation handled badly or failed to deliver. If there are patterns in this, corrective action can be taken. Regular exit polling can thus offer many benefits.

Commitment

Another piece of learning from the commercial world is that sometimes even very satisfied customers will quit. One day they will just decide to do business with someone else. What this tells us is that satisfaction, while important, is not the only underlying factor at work. Some customers will quit because, while they are satisfied, they lack any kind of commitment to the organisation. In our sector too, donors will lapse because while the service provided was OK, they are in no way committed to the charity.

So what is commitment? I define it as a genuine desire to maintain a relationship into the future. In the giving context it is a genuine passion for, or belief in what the organisation is trying to achieve. 'I really care about the work of this organisation.' It differs from satisfaction because satisfaction is an amalgam of past experience while commitment is forward looking in nature.

It turns out that in the nonprofit context there are actually two types of commitment, what I've labelled passive commitment and active commitment[2]. Active commitment is the enduring passion for the organisation I've just described. For nonprofits, the ability to inspire individuals by the work they undertake is key to building loyalty and yet so many organisations fail to successfully tell their story to donors. Work that could inspire others to share the organisation's passion for the mission is somehow lost in transmission.

The second category is passive commitment. This refers to individuals who continue their support not because they feel strongly about the work of the organisation, but because they feel it is the 'right thing to do'. The work doesn't excite them, but they know it's important. Passive commitment can also manifest in the realm of regular or sustained giving. Donors can look as though they are highly loyal, but in reality they are continuing their support only because they haven't got around to cancelling, or had actually forgotten they were still giving. Quite a few nonprofits with regular (or in the USA, 'sustained') gift programmes will notice a spike in attrition immediately after sending out a mailing. What they've done through the communication is to remind some folk who had forgotten they were still giving that they are in fact still doing so, and a small but significant percentage will rush out and cancel.

Keys to retention

So how do we prevent this? Active commitment is the key to retention and we know from research that there are a variety of factors that fundraisers can actively influence to drive this. The first of these is good old service quality. Not only does it have a direct impact on loyalty, it also helps build it indirectly by fostering commitment. If donors are treated well by the organisation they respond accordingly.

... the more likely I am to develop commitment and, through that, loyalty.

The second factor that drives commitment is the donor's perception of risk. To illustrate, if I am supporting a shelter for the homeless I am more likely to develop commitment if I forge a close link in my mind between my gift and the impact on the beneficiary. The stronger my belief that if I cancel my gift someone somewhere will be without a bed tonight, the more likely I am to develop commitment and, through that, loyalty. By contrast, if I believe that cancelling my gift won't make the slightest difference to the work the organisation is conducting the less likely I am to remain loyal. Fundraisers can therefore think through the messages they use in their appeals *and* the way in which they thank donors, to engender loyalty. Thank-you letters too can do a lot more than just acknowledge the gift, they can impress on donors the difference their donation has actually made.

Shared beliefs are the third factor of interest. Believing in the work of the organisation is one thing, but altogether more powerful is buying into its values. With many thousands of nonprofits all doing related things donors have a plethora of philanthropic choices. The issue in loyalty is therefore not only what do they do, but how do they do it and with what in mind. In other words, in building loyalty it is important to convince the donor not only of the quality of the work, but what the work will deliver for society. If I share your vision of the world you want to see and I share your vision of how this world will be delivered I will be a great deal more committed to your organisation than if I lack these perspectives. Of course you can't make someone share your beliefs, but you can be clear about them and use all your powers of persuasion to explain why you hold the views that you do and why others should join you. The more that donors buy into the beliefs of your organisation, the more loyal they will be.

Use of language

Personal links are also important. Intuitively one would expect that someone who has lost a loved one to breast cancer would be a good deal more committed, for example, to breast cancer charities as a consequence. This isn't at all surprising. A deep personal link to a cause can be a powerful stimulant to giving. Medical research charities, hospitals, hospices, etc. will all garner loyalty by virtue of personal links in a way that is difficult for others to emulate.

Well, that's not quite true. If they think about it, many nonprofits could do more to personalise the impact of the work they do. Is Greenpeace just preserving the environment, or is it preserving the environment for my children and my grandchildren to enjoy tomorrow? Does Cancer Research UK need my help to find a cure for cancer because 25 per cent of the UK population will be touched by cancer at some point in their lives, or do they need my help because one in four of my family and friends will be touched by the disease? It is perfectly possible to build up a sense of personal connection through the skilful use of language. For a masterclass in how to do this well I refer folks to George Smith's sublime book *Asking Properly* (The White Lion Press, 2004, www.whitelionpress.com).

A further factor in loyalty is the notion of 'multiple engagements'. This has two levels to it, one intuitive, one less so. The intuitive level is that donors who are also campaigners, who are also volunteers, who are also service users, etc, will be a good deal more loyal than those who are only one of these things. A good strategy is thus to encourage donors to support the organisation in multiple ways. With the advent of the internet and e-mail this is now beautifully simple to accomplish and at almost zero incremental cost.

The second level is not so obvious. Research tells us that each time an organisation has a two-way interaction with a donor it builds a little loyalty. As we discussed earlier, this interaction could take the form of a piece of research that asks donors for their views. It might offer them some choice over how they are communicated with (e.g. mail, e-mail, text) and how often. It might even give donors choice over the content of these communications, allowing donors to tailor them to their specific interests. Each time a donor has to think through a choice, or the provision of a piece of information she has to 'rehearse' in her mind the fact that she has a relationship with the organisation. Now she has to specify the form that this relationship will take. Each time she does this a tighter bond begins to evolve between her and the organisation concerned.

Smart strategy

The increases in loyalty each time are not huge, but over time they can become quite substantive. Investing in an ongoing dialogue with donors is therefore a smart strategy to adopt. Supporters can be asked to sign up for specific forms of communication, to offer recommendations or suggestions, to take part in research, to 'ask the expert', to campaign on behalf of the organisation, to 'test' their knowledge in a quiz, etc. The more two-way interactions that are engendered, the higher will be the level of loyalty achieved.

Choice

Offering donors choice is the key. When do you want to hear from us? What aspects of our work are you interested in? Would you like e-mail or regular mail? Are you interested in a newsletter, or a once a year update? Would you like news but not to be asked for money? All of these are questions that can be asked of donors with a view to personalising the relationship. It's smart because it moves the organisation from intrusion in direct marketing activity towards invitation. In effect donors are giving the organisation permission to communicate with them in a particular way at a particular time. This is formally known as permission marketing. Communications are then personalised and relevant to their needs. Little wonder that donors respond with higher levels of giving and enhanced levels of loyalty.

The final factor is learning. Fundraisers need to think through the journey that supporters will take as they deepen their understanding of the organisation and the mission it is trying to accomplish. Some sector luminaries now talk about planning 'supporter journeys' and my own research suggests this is important. If donors feel that the relationship they have with the organisation consists of a series of disjointed and unrelated requests for money they will be likely to quit. By definition, there is no relationship, we are just shouting at people. In contrast, those who feel that the organisation is taking them on a coordinated journey, designed to deepen their understanding of the cause and what needs to be accomplished, will be significantly more loyal. This doesn't prevent an organisation from sending an occasional emergency appeal as a need arises, but it does require the balance of communications to be planned rather than conducted on an ad hoc basis.

Allied to this latter point, some charities recruiting donors through direct marketing media, such as the mail, press advertising, direct dialogue (face-to-face), or through direct response television advertising have had success with welcome cycles. In other words, when donors are recruited they do not find themselves suddenly exposed to an organisation's routine pattern of communication. Rather, they are put into a tailored cycle of communication designed to educate and engage new donors. This might be as simple as a welcome call, or welcome pack. It may involve three or four communications designed specifically for new supporters, which will bring them up to speed with the work the organisation is trying to accomplish and why this is important. In the case of cash donors (individuals who routinely send cheques rather than sign up to a regular payment) a welcome cycle serves a further purpose, it encourages the all important second and third donation, which gets donors used to offering their support and develops their sense of identity as a supporter. For this reason the welcome cycle should comprise some of the organisation's strongest, most effective communications. In the context of direct mail this might involve appropriately tailored variants of the charity's best three or four donor recruitment packs.

This might be as simple as a welcome call, ..

Trust

Fundraisers have long recognised the significance of trust in building donor loyalty. I've been attending fundraising conventions for almost 20 years and every year speaker after speaker can be heard telling audiences about the importance of reporting back to donors exactly how their monies have been used. This is fundamental to successful fundraising. It turns out that it isn't the feedback that builds loyalty per se, rather the trust that this feedback engenders. As donors develop their trust in a nonprofit they will exhibit higher levels of loyalty.

So what do we mean by trust? Trust in this context is the belief on the part of a donor that their needs will be met in the future by the actions taken by the charity. They care about relieving suffering in the third world and because they can't see the relief work first hand, they must trust that Oxfam or an equivalent will deliver this effectively and efficiently. To build trust it is vital that when donors offer money for a specific purpose they are reassured after the event that that is exactly how the monies were used and provided with evidence of the impacts that resulted. To be effective it is important not to overdo this. We have probably all had letters along the lines of, 'Thank you Mr Bloggs for that fabulous gift of 20p. With your valuable donation we have quite literally changed the world.' This strains the boundaries of credibility and questions the donor's intelligence. To evoke trust the impacts achieved should be related (as far as possible) to the donor's actual donation and the content changed accordingly. Some form of segmentation is therefore necessary when thank-you or follow-up letters are drafted. They must be tailored and believable.

This is just one way to build trust. Fundraising research has shown that trust can also be built by:[3]

1. Being seen to exercise role competence

This is a fancy way of saying that fundraisers need to demonstrate that the organisation has the requisite skills and abilities to achieve its mission. Donors need to know that the organisation is equipped to do what it says it will do. They'll trust that Oxfam can relieve suffering when they understand the personnel, expertise, resources and infrastructure it can bring to bear in an emergency. They'll trust even more when they are shown how this has happened so successfully in the past. Similarly, a hospice must show that it has the right numbers of highly skilled and professional staff, that the environment is respectful of patients and their families, that patient dignity is routinely respected, that it provides consistently excellent standards of care, etc.

In building trust it isn't enough that these things are happening, they must be seen to be happening by all the organisation's supporters. When we design newsletters, fundraising copy, e-mail communications, etc. we need to provide donors with real evidence that our organisation is the best organisation to be providing the service, or tackling the issues our donors care about.

2. Drip feeding data on performance

Trust can also be built by providing ongoing cues as to the organisation's use of resources. Is the nonprofit well run, spending a high percentage of its income on the cause, tightly controlling costs, not paying its executives outrageous sums of money and so forth? Performance data can be drip fed into newsletters, campaign solicitations, press releases, website copy, etc. Supporters can even be provided with a contact that they can call or e-mail for information should they have any queries. The good news for fundraisers in this area is that donors actually have a very low level of expectations. They suspect, for example, that even the charities they care about are spending only 60 per cent of their income on programmes, when for most of our organisations the figure will actually be much higher. What donors want is actually pretty close to what most nonprofits already deliver.

3. Being honest when things go wrong

Most of the time charities can deliver exactly what they promised to donors in exactly the way they promised to deliver it. Sometimes though, even the best of us screw up. We handle something badly, or encounter unforeseen difficulties that complicate the provision of the service, or the attainment of a goal. If this is the case we know from research that trust can still be developed by being open and honest with the donor about the issues, the potential solutions and where the organisation will go from here.

There is no need to try and gloss over failure or only partial success. Aside from the fact that donors will find the honesty refreshing and respect you more as a consequence, it is often the case that the reasons for the only partial success are fascinating and can add real value for donors seeking to understand the complex challenges the organisation might face. It is an odd quirk of human behaviour that when people are willing to admit mistakes and seen to learn from them, they generate significantly higher levels of trust than if they'd got things right first time.

4. Being seen to exercise good judgement

Demonstrating that the organisation is having the envisaged impact is only part of the story. How the organisation goes about achieving this impact is also important. To what extent does the organisation act in a manner consistent with its stated values and principles in how it deals with beneficiaries, stewards resources, solicits funds and develops its campaigns? How these matters are handled is at least as important as what they deliver.

5. Adhering to appropriate standards of professional conduct

Being seen to subscribe to a code of conduct or code of professional ethics can also build trust. The act of signing up to the Fund Raising Standards Board (or equivalent) sends a strong message to donors about the professionalism of the fundraising team. Signing up to the 'fundraising promise' or, my personal favourite, the USA's Association of Fundraising Professionals' superb 'donor bill of

The donor bill of rights

Philanthropy is based on voluntary action for the common good. It is a tradition of giving and sharing that is primary to the quality of life. To ensure that philanthropy merits the respect and trust of the general public, and that donors and prospective donors can have full confidence in the nonprofit organizations and causes they are asked to support, we declare that all donors have these rights:

I. To be informed of the organization's mission, of the way the organization intends to use donated resources, and of its capacity to use donations effectively for their intended purposes.

II. To be informed of the identity of those serving on the organization's governing board, and to expect the board to exercise prudent judgment in its stewardship responsibilities.

III. To have access to the organization's most recent financial statements.

IV. To be assured their gifts will be used for the purposes for which they were given.

V. To receive appropriate acknowledgement and recognition.

VI. To be assured that information about their donation is handled with respect and with confidentiality to the extent provided by law.

VII. To expect that all relationships with individuals representing organizations of interest to the donor will be professional in nature.

VIII. To be informed whether those seeking donations are volunteers, employees of the organization or hired solicitors.

IX. To have the opportunity for their names to be deleted from mailing lists that an organization may intend to share.

X. To feel free to ask questions when making a donation and to receive prompt, truthful and forthright answers.

Source: Association of Fundraising Professionals (2009a). Reproduced with kind permission.

rights' does likewise. Such things illustrate that the organisation does indeed care about its supporters and takes its responsibilities towards them seriously. There may be similar principles of codes or practice that are appropriate to the service the nonprofit provides to beneficiaries and, again, promotion of their adoption will also build trust.

6. Development of a complaints procedure

Many of the codes we allude to above require that an organisation establishes and promotes an appropriate complaints handling procedure. The existence of such a scheme and its promotion, whether individuals choose to avail themselves of it or not, will likewise bolster trust.

Identity and
identification

The big three drivers of loyalty are satisfaction, trust and commitment. We now understand enough about these factors to be able to actively manage them, therefore ensuring that our communications meet donor needs in all three regards. The preceding chapters are packed with practical steps that organisations can take to bolster loyalty, but before leaving the subject of the underlying drivers of loyalty completely there is one further factor that warrants our attention. It is a little more esoteric than the previous three, but very powerful nonetheless.

Research taking place in psychology, economics and marketing has recently explored how the essence of *whom* we are drives what we choose to support. Causes and organisations that more closely align with our sense of self-identity will tend to attract higher levels of loyalty from us than those that do not. This is true of both membership and non-membership contexts. When a person identifies with an organisation, he or she perceives a sense of connectedness with it and begins to define him or herself (at least in part) in terms of the supported organisation.

When she gives she is acting out these identities and feels good about herself...

As an example, someone might give to Greenpeace because she sees herself as a Greenpeace supporter, an environmental campaigner, a responsible parent saving the environment for her children to enjoy, or just someone who cares about the environment, whales, deforestation, climate change, etc. When she gives she is acting out these identities and feels good about herself because the identity itself is reinforced. Following through on this example, Greenpeace can make me feel good about my support by reassuring me that I'm being a responsible parent, safeguarding my child's future, when I send them a gift.

Equally, when I support the Royal British Legion in November I may give because I was formerly a part of the armed services, part of the wider services family, or more commonly because I want to be seen as someone who honours and respects the service of others. So powerful has this latter identity become in the UK that in the run up to Remembrance Sunday every celebrity, newscaster, politician, or person of influence in the media will be seen wearing a poppy and sharing in this collective persona.

Concept of identity

Although we are just beginning to quantify the effects of identity on giving, the idea is not new. As long ago as 1959, one of the great marketing gurus Sidney Levy noted that people buy things not only for what they do, but also for what they mean. People are drawn to charities that are perceived as having a personality congruent to their own, be it actual or aspired. This last point is important, giving can reflect not only who donors are, but also who they would like to become. Just as in the commercial world where consumers are loyal to brands that in some sense they aspire to, so too will donors continue to give to organisations that support their sense of who they would like to be.

So how can fundraisers make use of the concept of identity to build loyalty?

In the US, Jen Shang (an assistant professor at Indiana University) and I recently conducted an experiment with supporters of public radio. Unlike the UK where public broadcasting is supported by a licence fee, in America it is supported in large measure by public donations or subscriptions. As a consequence each station has one or two on air campaigns each year designed to raise funds. What typically happens is that an appeal total is set for each hour of broadcasting and listeners are invited to call in and make or renew a donation.

... significantly increased the amount they were willing to donate.

In our study individuals who called in to make a donation were asked how much they identified themselves with the station. We found that the more donors identified themselves with the station, the more they were likely to give larger amounts. This is the lower line on the graph in figure 3. Interestingly, priming that identification, by asking people about it directly *before* they offered their gift, significantly increased the amount they were willing to donate. The upper of the two lines in figure 3 illustrates this. If fundraisers can encourage people to think through their identification with the

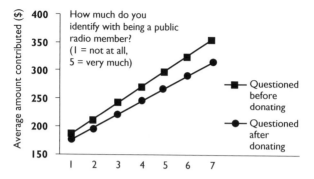

Figure 3: The effect of donor identification on donation level

organisation they will increase giving and increase it quite substantially. To be most effective this needs to happen immediately before they are asked to specify the amount they will donate, or the level of their upgrade.

Many charities routinely attempt to build up donors' feelings of identification with their organisation. They want donors to begin to see their support of the organisation as a critical part of who they are and deliberately attempt to foster this over time. As we can see from the graph this is a smart strategy. Donors with higher levels of identification give more – a lot more. There also turns out to be a relationship between the degree of identification felt by the donor and how likely they are to still be giving next year. Identification builds giving and it also builds loyalty.

What our work suggests is that, to be most

effective, priming identity needs to happen in a structured way with adequate consideration given to both relevance and salience. In other words donors need to be *reminded* why the identity is important to them and the relevance it has to who they are. If the goal is to increase giving this needs to be front of mind as they read the solicitation and, ideally, right before they select the amount of their donation. If the goal is to build loyalty this reflection should be regularly encouraged in ongoing communication.

Of course this is a very global approach. Identification with Greenpeace or public radio means something to donors. Both organisations have strong and very visible personalities. What it might mean to have identification with, say, the University of Exeter would be less clear. In this case it makes much more sense to look at individual identities that might be important, rather than identification with the organisation per se. I might give because I identify with current or past students, with a celebrity endorser, faculty, a favoured professor, or a particular department. I might even give because I identify myself as a resident of Exeter and see the university as essential for the well being of my local community. These separate identities can be primed in fundraising communications in exactly the same way as identification with the organisation as a whole. As a consequence it is essential that a charity develops an understanding of the complex web of identities that might be important to donors and reflects this in the way that language is used in appeals.

We should also be thinking about the language we use in our acknowledgements and thank yous. We frequently thank people for their 'kind' and 'generous' donations and thus routinely confer these identities to our supporters. There is a good deal of evidence that wanting to be seen as a moral person is a critical identity for many donors so the use of these words is a smart strategy to adopt. This is a pretty limited approach though. There may be other more powerful identities that the donor could be reminded of and feel even better about as a consequence. Relevant identities should be primed in newsletters, solicitations and thank-you notes and, to maximise their effect, be developed consistently over time.

... the beauty here is that it can do so at no additional cost.

I said at the outset of this chapter that the concept of identity is a little more esoteric than the concepts we have discussed previously. This is true, but hopefully I have also demonstrated what a powerful tool it can be to both stimulate donations and foster loyalty. Knowledge of the psychology underlying giving can be used to great effect in enhancing the performance of fundraising and the beauty here is that it can do so at no additional cost. We are talking only about the skilful use of language. It is also important to stress that we are not using this knowledge to manipulate donors, but rather to help them maximise the benefit they personally derive from their giving. A knowledge of identity helps create a series of win-win exchanges that not only build loyalty, but also make donors feel genuinely good about their giving.

Avoid activities that
damage loyalty

So far in this text we have been looking at the factors that build loyalty. In this chapter we will move on to consider ways in which nonprofits can unwittingly destroy it. Chief among these is the all too common practice of list swaps or, in UK fundraising speak, 'reciprocal' mailings. In an age when we are concerned about the costs of fundraising and reporting that we spend only 20 pence (or similar) to raise a pound, it isn't at all surprising that organisations look for the cheapest ways to do things and, as I've already mentioned, one of the most significant costs a fundraiser will face is the cost of acquisition. So anything that can help a nonprofit lower its cost of acquisition has to be a good thing – right?

Wrong. When I last conducted a benchmarking exercise of direct marketing activity in fundraising I was horrified to discover just how prevalent reciprocal or list swap mailings had become. Attempts to bring in genuinely new donors to the sector appear now to be the exception rather than the norm. Charities adopting the reciprocal approach do so for the very good reason that they can often turn what would otherwise have been a loss in donor recruitment into a breakeven position, or better. Reciprocals are a relatively cheap form of recruitment.

There are, however, a number of difficulties with this approach. No one in their right mind swaps their high value donors, so the individuals swapped tend to be low value. If they appear as a low value donor on one organisation's database they will probably appear as a low value donor on another's. As a consequence they can find themselves input to swaps by multiple organisations. To illustrate this point a typical direct mail donor presently supports an average of around five charities. By contrast a typical reciprocal donor supports an average of 11 to 12. They give to a bewildering array of different organisations, very few of which will be able to garner anything approaching real donor loyalty as a consequence. How can an organisation even begin to get its message across amid all this clutter?

Frustration, even anger

Imagine the communications these folks receive. Assuming that they support only around 10 per cent of the organisations that solicit them this means that they receive around a hundred solicitation letters each year. To this you can add the development solicitations from the organisations they do support, for argument's sake five to six communications including newsletters, catalogues and the like. This brings the total up to closer to 170, or almost one communication for every two days of the year. Little wonder then that individuals complain about the volume of communication they receive from nonprofits. Not only do reciprocal mailings destroy loyalty they also damage the public's trust.

In fairness there are sector agencies that try to manage the reciprocal process, working with their clients to try to limit a given individual's exposure to solicitation. Such agencies have an enormous database of donors put into a common pool by participating charities. Specific individuals are thus selected for contact on an infrequent basis. Even here though many donors may not have realised they had given their permission to be swapped, therefore, creating frustration and even anger. Many more might be swapped directly with other nonprofits not participating in aggregate schemes. Try building loyalty when your supporters are actively being encouraged to broaden their portfolio. It doesn't work.

For the sake of completeness, there are two other issues I have with reciprocals. The first is that research has indicated that once a donor is swapped by a nonprofit her value to the organisation will fall by an average of 10 to 15 per cent thereafter.[4] The second is that research in the domain of legacies has illustrated that many low value givers are low value givers because they are cash poor, but quite possibly asset rich. While some donors may not be in a position to give large sums of money during their lifetime, if they are loyal supporters they will be significantly more likely to consider a legacy. Organisations swapping donors may therefore be jeopardising their chances of securing a gift in their will. One of the single biggest determinants of whether someone will leave a legacy is the duration of their lifetime support.

... if they are loyal supporters they will be significantly more likely to consider a legacy.

Begin to factor all these additional losses into the cost benefit analysis of whether or not to engage in recruitment from reciprocal lists and you can begin to see why this is no longer such an easy decision. Factor in too the 'costs' associated with irritating donors with excessive communication and the decision becomes even more difficult. I am certainly not suggesting that all charities should avoid reciprocals, just that the maths involved in reaching the decision should be altogether more sophisticated. The bottom line here is that actively encouraging donors to support other organisations is one sure way to kill loyalty.

I did mention there were others. I remember reading in *Third Sector* magazine in the UK just recently of a donor who had been bombarded with free pairs of socks, an umbrella, T-shirts and all kinds of other assorted items in a bid by multiple organisations to win his support. He was pictured alongside quite literally a table full of such correspondence that he had received over the course of the year. Wasteful was one of the words he used in his description. They probably couldn't print the others.

Perceived expenses

As we have already seen, donors will assume that organisations wasteful of their fundraising expenditure will also be wasteful in terms of how they use their money in service provision. Loyalty is hit as a consequence. As insiders we might know that the inclusion of these items will probably have been tested and found to produce a higher return on investment, but the average donor doesn't know this. They just see that you've sent them an umbrella or a coin of the realm. It looks and feels expensive, whatever the rights or wrongs of the specific case.

The perceived expense isn't the only issue. Gifts, premiums, or involvement devices are frequently used, particularly for new donor acquisition; they are designed to stimulate and interest the donor and prompt them into making a gift. The key to success lies in the selection of items that are appropriate. Low cost yes, but also items that are intrinsically linked to the cause. What relevance has an umbrella to an animal welfare charity, or a pair of socks to a hospice? The most effective involvement devices are those that have value only because it is a particular charity that has sent it.

I can vividly remember receiving a communication from Sense some years ago (a UK charity for deaf/blind people) and in particular a letter for their holiday appeal. The organisation was looking to send deaf/blind children on a vacation, offering a chance for them to discover and explore the world around them. Inside the envelope was a simple drinking straw – a child's memory, we were told, of a holiday past. It is only on reading the communication that you begin to realise what it looks like to view the world from the perspective of a deaf/blind child and the straw became a very powerful representation of what they were trying to achieve. Not only was this a wonderfully warm and thought provoking communication, it was incredibly smart from a loyalty perspective. Items intrinsically linked to the cause are many times more powerful than those that are not.

The same is true in the realm of major gifts. Charities offer many different kinds of recognition to high value donors, including plaques, paperweights and other assorted paraphernalia, but none of these are intrinsically linked to the cause. None of them build loyalty. Gifts linked to the cause do. Should UNICEF thank a major donor by sending her a paperweight, or would they do better to send a crayon drawing from a grateful child in a village she has helped to save?

In the United States some public radio stations reward donors for giving at higher levels with gifts and premiums. They can even offer discounts at local restaurants or at local traders in return for the gift. This destroys donor loyalty because it builds up loyalty to the premium rather than loyalty to the organisation. Over time it also trains donors to expect a premium and eventually persuades them they're engaging in an economic exchange not a heartfelt one. A much smarter strategy to adopt would be, for example, to offer CDs of music or thought linked to the programming and thus only obtainable from public radio. This reminds people of the value they receive from the station and strengthens the bond.

Recruit loyal supporters in the first place

M odern technology is a wonderful thing. While analysing a database used to be a highly complex and specialist affair, rudimentary profiling is now within the reach of most fundraisers and fundraising budgets. Many of us have become used to planning a recruitment campaign by profiling our database, getting a sense of who supports us now and then using this profile to go out and find others that match it. The logic is simple; if a certain type of person has tended to support us in the past it will probably be cheaper to approach other similar kinds of people in the future. Statistically they would be more likely to have an interest in what we do and to respond with a donation as a consequence.

With the passage of time we have also been able to take profiling to the next level and look at the specific profiles of donors we recruit from direct mail, press advertising, direct response television and so on. In this

... if they are loyal supporters they will be significantly more likely to consider a legacy.

way a more refined profile is developed of donors most likely to respond to a given media. We have even wised up to the fact that not every donor will be of equal value and that the old-fashioned global profiles of supporters tended to be weighted towards that of the large volume of low value supporters at the bottom end of the database. Organisations are now able to look at the profile of higher value givers and to compare this with their lower value givers. If there should be differences they can be built into the criteria that will be used to target potential new donors.

Despite all this analysis, one form of analysis that hasn't occurred to many nonprofits is to look at the profile of loyal donors (i.e. not just high value donors) and to use this to define the audience for new donor acquisition. It's a simple point, but often neglected. If we can recruit individuals who are more likely to be loyal we can cut down on the number of donors we lose and save significantly on our future costs of recruitment.

In passing I should also mention that the same holds true for attempts to reactivate lapsed donors. Some charities routinely write to their lapsed file in the hope of reactivating past supporters. If they do this well, they will probably very successfully reactivate individuals who will give them only one further donation before disappearing again into oblivion. A more thoughtful approach would be to look at the profile of these individuals and to target only those who are likely to exhibit higher levels of loyalty and thus a higher lifetime value if they are successfully reactivated. Yes, we might have to work a little harder to re-engage with some of these folks, but if we save cost by not writing to everyone in the file this is perfectly do-able.

Too many fundraisers use simple return on investment models to select where and how they invest in recruiting new donors, or reactivating old ones. As a sector we must get more focused on how these folks will behave *after* we've recruited them. If they will only give once and then be lost to us forever, the initial ROI might look pretty good, but the lifetime return on investment will be lousy. Taking decisions with an eye to the longer term would have a profound effect on loyalty.

Anything else?

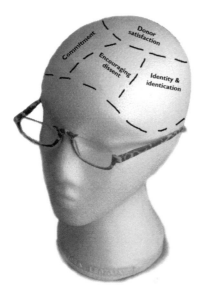

This is my catch-all chapter. A set of simple points that in isolation wouldn't warrant a chapter of their own, but that in aggregate are well worth considering. How else can you build loyalty?

1. Foster regular or sustained giving

The economics of regular giving are very different to those of recruiting and developing cash donors. It usually costs more to recruit regular givers because the decision to support is by definition more committed and involving. However, once recruited, regular givers exhibit much higher levels of loyalty. Instead of losing 50 per cent of these folks between their first and second donation we might lose only 15 to 20 per cent between year one and year two. Younger donors are significantly more comfortable with regular giving than their older counterparts, so offering regular giving, particularly as an online giving option, also has the potential to greatly increase the lifetime value of the supporter base. Longer-term relationships become possible.

2. Look carefully at the case for support you employ

If your organisation experiences a high level of attrition between the first and second donation (or in the early months of regular giving) look carefully at the messages that are being used to recruit donors and the messages the organisation uses to engage with them thereafter. Some nonprofits use very different messages, often in larger organisations because different teams are responding for the different categories of appeal. As a consequence donors are initially encouraged to give for one reason and then exposed to communications that expect them to give for another. The approach needs to be integrated and consistent.

3. Reactivate lapsed donors with the messages that recruited them originally

If your organisation has fallen into the trap outlined above you may find considerable utility in looking back over the messages that have historically been used for new donor acquisition. These messages can be the best messages to use to re-engage with supporters who have subsequently lapsed. Beware though – if there is still a disconnect between the recruitment and development side of your fundraising equation you may find yourself reactivating people only to lose them once more.

4. Ask donors what interests them

When new donors are recruited, or shortly thereafter, consider asking them which aspects of your organisation's work are more interesting to them. Perhaps identify four to six categories of activity (through research) and allow donors to specify one or all of their interests. This information can then be captured and used to drive the communications they will receive in future, or at the very least the balance of content in newsletters and magazines. With the advent of the internet and e-mail it should be possible, at very low cost, to operate some degree of segmentation that engages the donors' real interests.

5. Recognise that donors come in all shapes and sizes

What I mean here is that donors recruited from one medium can be very different from donors who are recruited from another. Equally donors who are recruited into regular giving will be very different from donors who send only occasional cheques.

Despite these differences some nonprofits have historically had only a one-size-fits-all approach to donor development. Donors recruited into cash giving from direct mail may be 40 or more years older than a cohort of donors recruited into regular giving by direct dialogue, or face-to-face. It makes no sense that they would have the same interests, or respond well to an identical pattern of communication. One of the reasons for the historically high levels of attrition among donors recruited by direct dialogue was that many charities subsequently sent these 30-somethings the same communications they were sending to their 80-year-olds.

6. Examine a 'Year in the Life Of'

Don't assume that the only communications your donors receive have been written by you. They may have been, but equally they may not have been. Internal lists could have been shared with fundraisers in other teams, or with other sections of the organisation such as the service provision or campaigning team. It can therefore be instructive to see what it feels like to be a supporter of your own organisation. Add your own name to the database and find out. Do the communications you receive all give the same impression of the organisation and build to a coherent whole, or is it a miscellany of obviously uncoordinated material?

7. Remember that everything communicates

I have stressed in earlier chapters how important the values of the organisation can be in building loyalty. Communicating these consistently can help build commitment and assist in fostering identification. Don't assume that only fundraising communications have the power to communicate. Newsletters, website design, copy and ambience, e-mail, telephone conversations with staff/volunteers, face-to-face presentations, annual reports, letters from employees/volunteers, press releases, etc. can all communicate. Organisations that consistently manage all these 'touch points' with the organisation's brand will fare much better at communicating the charity's values and convincing donors of why these are important.

8. Use the language of loyalty

My final point is aimed squarely at nonprofits on the American side of the Atlantic. Fundraising in that context has traditionally been conducted to support the annual fund, capital campaigns, endowments and planned giving. We've been hung up on campaigns for over a century. Remember that donors don't give to support campaigns they give to support need. It therefore makes more sense to adopt an integrated approach to how you address donors, talking to them about aspects of your work that interest them and then exploring how the gift will be administered. It also makes sense to move away from language that encourages donors to believe that they have only a series of annual transactions with the nonprofit and not a relationship. Whatever we might choose to call it internally, the very notion of an annual fund is an anathema to loyalty. We should drop all mention of an annual fund in our solicitations and instead focus on need and developing an ongoing relationship, not transactions, with our donors.

Conclusions

We have covered a lot of ground in this text, beginning by exploring the difference that even small improvements in loyalty can make to the longer-term value of the fundraising database. Adopting even a few of the ideas in this book could thus make a very big difference to the performance of your organisation.

We began our discussion of how to achieve loyalty by focusing on the underlying factors that drive it. I encouraged you to pay particular attention to the quality of service provided not to your beneficiaries, but rather to the donor by your fundraising team. I also encouraged you to think at the conceptual level and to consider the quality of service as a whole rather than focusing on a handful of specifics. To do so would be dangerous because donors form a holistic view of relationships and dissatisfaction in any one area can taint the overall perspective.

We also discussed the notion of commitment, noting that even highly satisfied donors will sometimes stop supporting you because they lack this additional bond to the organisation. We explored a whole series of different ways in which organisations can look to build commitment. What is notable about this list is that the majority of the suggestions offered could be integrated into an organisation's strategy at almost zero incremental cost. We have frequently talked about changes only to the language that is used in solicitation and ongoing communication. Skilful manipulation of words can result in gains for both the donor and the organisation.

Nowhere was this truer than in the domain of identification. While the research base here is nowhere near as well developed as in other areas, it is clear that many donors offer their support because they view this as part of who they are. In effect they express one or more identities *through* their giving. Nonprofits seeking to keep their donors should therefore reflect on the various identities that supporters might have and how the organisation could seek to reinforce and add value to these through their fundraising and other communications. Aiding donors to foster a favourable image of themselves is yet a further route to developing loyalty.

In closing I would like to stress that each of the points I make in this book have been substantiated through prior research. The points I make are not a matter of my own personal opinion, or the experience of one isolated nonprofit, they are based on over 20 years of work by researchers working in the fields of psychology, sociology, economics and marketing. There is now a wealth of information that could and should be making a difference to our professional practice. There is no longer any reason to accept the appallingly high levels of attrition the sector has experienced to date. The path to resolving this is clear and I commend it to you.

Further reading

[1] Jones, T.O and Sasser W.E. (1995) 'Why Satisfied Customers Defect', *Harvard Business Review,* Nov/Dec, 88–99.

[2] Sargeant A and Woodliffe L (2007) 'Building Donor Loyalty: The Antecedents and Role of Commitment in the Context of Charity Giving', *Journal of Nonprofit and Public Sector Marketing,* 18(2), 47–68.

[3] Sargeant A and Lee S (2002) 'Individual and Contextual Antecedents of Donor Trust in the Voluntary Sector', *Journal of Marketing Management,* 18(7–8), pp779–802.

[4] Sargeant A and Jay E (2004) *Building Donor Loyalty: The Fundraiser's Guide to Increasing Lifetime Value,* Jossey Bass, San Francisco.

About the
'Tiny Essentials' series

The book you hold in your hands is part of a series of little books with a big mission. They focus on what really matters in one key area of voluntary sector management. Each book's purpose is to provide the essentials of its subject in an entertaining, easily digestible form, so people who otherwise wouldn't dream of reading a business book can effortlessly and enjoyably get access to what they really need to know.

Books in the 'Tiny Essentials' series are delightfully free of padding, waffle and over-blown theories. Extraneous material has been reduced to a minimum. Each book so lives up to its title that there's just no room for anything other than the essence of what really matters in the subject area, and how to order your priorities.

This 'Tiny' focuses on what every fundraiser, CEO and board member needs to know about preparing and implementing a fundraising strategy. Other books in the 'Tiny' series are:

Tiny Essentials of Fundraising, by Neil Sloggie

Tiny Essentials of Writing for Fundraising, by George Smith

Tiny Essentials of Major Gift Fundraising, by Neil Sloggie

Tiny Essentials of an Effective Volunteer Board, by Ken Burnett

Tiny Essentials of Raising Money from Foundations and Trusts, by Jo Habib

Tiny Essentials of Monthly Committed Giving, by Harvey McKinnon

Tiny Essentials of a Fundraising Strategy, by Maggie Taylor and Ilene Hoyle

All can be ordered at www.whitelionpress.com

A promise from
The White Lion Press

Enjoy the best books on fundraising and voluntary sector development. Books by The White Lion Press will repay your investment many times over – and you'll enjoy reading them too. But if your purchase is damaged in any way, or if you feel any of our products do not live up to your expectations simply return them to us and we will issue you with a full refund, including any reasonable associated costs. We'll ask you to tell us why, so we can put right anything that might be wrong, but we won't quibble. Unfortunately we can only offer this if you bought the book directly from us, but even if you didn't, please let us know your problem and we'll do all we can to ensure your supplier matches our commitment to you. After all, you are our ultimate customer.

We further promise to handle your orders with speed, efficiency and impressive politeness.

You can order further copies of this book, or any of our other titles, from our secure website, www.whitelionpress.com.

If you prefer, you can order by email, orders@whitelionpress.com.

Tiny Essentials of Fundraising

by Neil Sloggie
Softback, 57 pp. ISBN 0-9518971-5-2

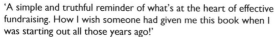

All you really need to know about
fundraising, in one tiny book.

Join Kate, an inquisitive and ambitious
new recruit to the fundraising
profession, as she sets out to uncover
what really matters in her chosen
career by visiting and asking three
seasoned practitioners. Like Kate
you'll see as much to avoid as to emulate in
the first two encounters but you'll be reassured and
inspired as, in her final meeting, Kate discovers an
organisation that has really thought through its fundraising
strategy and approach, and shares with her – and you – the
essential secrets of fundraising success.

'A simple and truthful reminder of what's at the heart of effective
fundraising. How I wish someone had given me this book when I
was starting out all those years ago!'
Jan Chisholm, managing director, Pareto Fundraising, Australia.

'I was given a copy of the "Tiny" book in Australia and was so
enamoured of the clear message it conveys that I ordered a special
edition to give to more than 1,500 fundraisers and all 700 Blackbaud
employees. Their reactions have been universally positive. *Tiny
Essentials of Fundraising* is one of those books that make us truly
envious of the author for executing such a brilliant piece of
writing...'
Robert Sywolski, chief executive, Blackbaud Inc, USA.

'It's a smart idea, well-executed – how fabulous to have a bite-sized
book that sums up what makes for successful fundraising in such an
accessible way to both native and non-native English speakers.

'Great stuff. Thanks Neil for what must be the shortest, simplest
and yet very salient contribution to the world's literature on
fundraising.'
Julie Weston, deputy executive director, fundraising, UNICEF UK.

Tiny Essentials of Writing for Fundraising

by George Smith
Softback, 65 pp.
ISBN 0-9518971-6-0

'I suggest your heart would soar if – once in a while – you received a letter written in decent English which said unexpected things in elegant ways, which moved you and stirred your emotions, which angered you or made you proud, a letter apparently written by one individual to another individual. For you never see these letters any more…'

If you believe that words matter then this opinionated little book is for you. For this 'Tiny' book will change forever the way you and your organisation communicate.

'*Tiny Essentials of Writing for Fundraising* is a refreshing – and delightfully short – guide to the author's insights about the writer's craft. If you're even thinking about writing fundraising letters you can't afford not to buy this remarkable little book.'
Mal Warwick, chairman, Mal Warwick & Associates Inc, USA.

'I am a huge fan of George's blunt but refined writing, his clear and individual voice, and his extraordinary ability to cut through the crap – keep this wonderful little book next to your pen and pc.'
Lyndall Stein, CEO, Concern, UK.

'Smith is a self-confessed curmudgeon but nobody describes better than he the power of words to advance your cause. The 11,149 words in this lovely book have been carefully selected and assembled to help you write well enough to convince anyone of anything.'
Ken Burnett, author, *The Zen of Fundraising*, UK.

Tiny Essentials of Major Gift Fundraising

by Neil Sloggie
Softback, 61 pp. ISBN 0-9518971-7-9

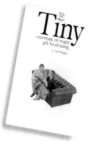

The natural successor to his first book,
Tiny Essentials of Fundraising, this
time Neil Sloggie tells the story of
Daniel, who had never thought of
asking any donor individually for
money, nor of asking for more than
a three-figure sum. Join him in his
search to uncover the Holy Grail of
major gift fundraising and learn as he did how
to secure donations bigger than a house – and lots of them.

This 'Tiny' contains in their purest, most distilled form the
priceless secrets of a neglected area of vast fundraising potential.

'Help is close at hand in this small gem – wise counsel, the
importance of colleagues and networking, heaps of practical advice.
To borrow Neil's words, "keep this one near the top of your
priority pile".'
Sue-Anne Wallace, chief executive officer, Fundraising Institute-
Australia.

'… a really helpful guide, especially to someone just starting out or
wishing to do a quick reappraisal of their operation.'
Nick Booth, campaign director, NSPCC 'Full Stop' campaign, UK.

Tiny Essentials of an Effective Volunteer Board

by Ken Burnett
Softback, 81 pp. ISBN 0-9518971-8-7

When Warren Maxwell is suddenly propelled into the chairman's seat of the voluntary organisation on whose board he serves, he decides that his somewhat mediocre board is going to become a paragon of all that's excellent in nonprofit governance. Join him on his brief, eventful, enlightening quest to discover what makes a balanced, progressive and highly effective volunteer board.

'This excellent and very readable book is essential for every board member of a charity. I realise how much better a chair and trustee I could have been if only the book had been written 30 years earlier.'
Lord Joel Joffe, former chair of trustees, Oxfam UK and chair, The Giving Campaign, UK.

'This tiny book is a huge contribution to the literature on governing boards. Told as a compelling story, the insights and experience-based facts are woven skilfully throughout. A delight to read, the lessons fly off the page.'
Kay Sprinkel Grace, author, *Beyond Fundraising* and *The Ultimate Board Member's Book*, USA.

'This energising, readable book draws out what's really important, the true "tiny essentials". The 21 keys summarised in chapter six are the cream on the cake…'
Noerine Kaleeba, chair of trustees, ActionAid International, South Africa.

'This little book is absolutely brilliant; it's easy to read and is full of useful information on how to improve the effectiveness of trustee boards.

'I found this book to be a very informative resource. I loved the style; to have a fictional story to read certainly drove home the salient points far more than a dull, factual text could have done and I found this approach to be very warm and engaging.'
Tracy Saunders, information officer, in *Volunteering Magazine* July 2006, UK.

'In every field there are those who become the "philosophers" of their fields. Burnett is such a philosopher for the field of fundraising. He is, in essence, a "guru".

'Burnett's new book is appropriate for his status as fundraising guru
since it exhibits the wisdom and in-depth thinking that is
characteristic of one who is steeped in the history, philosophy, and
literature of the field.'

Joanne Fritz, in a review on the website Nonprofit Charitable Orgs (part
of the New York Times Group) August 2006, USA.

Tiny Essentials of Raising Money from Foundations and Trusts

by Jo Habib
Softback, 77 pp.
ISBN 0-9518971-9-5

Of all the world's major donors (and
they are major, giving away £33 billion
plus each year in the UK and USA
alone), foundations and trusts may be
the most pure. They have no
function other than to give their
money away. In *Tiny Essentials of
Raising Money from Foundations and
Trusts*, Jo Habib shows you with precision how
to get your share.

'This book brings clarity to a world that is often apparently obscure
and will help anyone understand the steps that need to be taken
when approaching others for money. Written clearly and simply it
will be invaluable both to the novice and to experienced old hands
who think they really understand their target market. It is definitely
essential reading.'

Julia Unwin, consultant and author, *The Grant-Making Tango*, UK.

'This is an encyclopaedia on fundraising from foundations and trusts
packed into a tiny book. Jo Habib covers everything a new
fundraiser will need to know, with admirable clarity, thoroughness
and authority. Experienced fundraisers should also refer to this
splendid guide, using it as a check list against which to review their
own practice.'

David Carrington, consultant, UK.

Tiny Essentials of Monthly Committed Giving

by Harvey McKinnon
Softback, 70 pp.
ISBN-13: 978-0-9553993-0-5;
ISBN-10: 0-9553993-0-0

This book clearly describes the secrets of committed giving, what they are and what they require. In an entertaining, readable yet practical way the author shares his insights, experience and wisdom. You can start by benefiting from this simple yet superbly effective fundraising proposition in not much longer than the 60 minutes or so it will take you to read this book.

'I read this "Tiny book" on the bus and made heads turn by laughing out loud several times. It is easy to read, easy to understand and will be easy to use since the 43 best ideas are summed up at the end. Veteran fundraiser Harvey McKinnon even gives you the answers to convince your mule of a boss that it is time to try monthly giving, now.'
Joan Flanagan, author, *Successful Fundraising*, USA.

'Everyone has time to read a tiny book and after you read this one, you'll be able to raise lots more money for your cause through setting up a monthly donor program. This is one of the best uses of an hour that I can think of.'
Rosemary Oliver, development director, Amnesty International, Canada.

'Harvey McKinnon's latest book is a kind of bedtime story for sleepless adults – those who run financially-strapped nonprofits. If you read it tonight, you'll sleep more peacefully. Tomorrow, you'll start raising more money.'
Andy Robinson, author, *Big Gifts for Small Groups and Grassroots Grants*, USA.

'This tiny guide has given philanthropy a huge gift. McKinnon's entertaining style whilst sharing his formidable fundraising skills is in itself an act of selfless generosity.'
Lelei LeLaulu, president, Counterpart International; chairman, Foundation of the Peoples of the South Pacific, Canada.

Tiny Essentials of a Fundraising Strategy

by Maggie Taylor and Ilene Hoyle
Softback, 80 pp.
ISBN-13: 978-0-9553993-2-9
ISBN-10: 0-9553993-2-7

Strategy scares people because it
sounds like it should involve
something substantial, like a war or
at last an invasion. But at its heart
strategy is just knowing where you
want to get to and working out the best
way to get there.

In this Tiny book Maggie Taylor and Ilene Hoyle have stripped
away all the mystique and mystery, replacing it with a logical
and straightforward account of why a sound strategy matters,
how you can go about getting one and how you can make sure it
works for you and your organisation.

'A small book full of big fundraising questions – with answers on
every page. A must read for those responsible for fundraising
strategy in small and large organisations.'
Jo Swinhoe, director of fundraising and marketing, Alzheimer's Society,
UK.

'This takes the fear out of the challenges of fundraising planning and
strategy with a worked example fundraisers everywhere can relate
to. Another Tiny guide that punches above its weight.'
Adrian Sargeant, Robert F Hartsook Professor of Fundraising, Indiana
University-Purdue University, USA.

'Short, simple and effective. A pain free way to think about developing and implementing your fundraising strategy.'
Jonathan Grapsas, regional director, Pareto Fundraising, Canada.

Free Degrees: How to fund your own education without debt

by Lyndi Smith
Softback, 96pp.
ISBN 978-0-9553993-1-2

**Your initial investment: £6.95.
Your potential return: up to
£26.000.**

Contrary to what many believe, education doesn't have to come at a price. Anyone can raise the funds necessary to pay their way through academic life, without getting into debt.

Without any prior experience, former drama student Lyndi Smith constructed a fundraising campaign that raised over £26,000. In Free Degrees Lyndi explains what it takes to raise money to pay for education start to finish.

'Sound and inspiring advice, as welcome to the penniless student as to the penniless actor. Bravo!'
Emma Thompson, Oscar-winning actress and screenwriter, UK.

'... really useful... astute, entertaining and very, very helpful. It offers first-class advice... Lyndi Smith makes fundraising sound like having fun.'
Professor Susan Bassnett, pro-vice chancellor and professor of comparative literature, University of Warwick, UK.

'... a life saver for teenagers about to launch into higher education – and their cash-strapped parents. Lyndi, you could be saving us thousands of pounds. Thank you.'
Jane Fricker, parent, UK.

The Zen of Fundraising

by Ken Burnett
Published by Jossey-Bass Inc in
association with The White Lion Press
Limited. Softback, 169 pp.
ISBN 978-0-7879-8314-7

If all that has ever been said and
written about the art and science of
fundraising could be distilled down to
just what really matters there would
be only a small number of true gems
deserving of the description 'nuggets of
information'.

Ken Burnett has identified and defined 89 such nuggets that he
presents here as *The Zen of Fundraising* – a fun-to-read, one-of-
a-kind look into what makes donors tick and, more importantly,
what makes them give.

'Ken Burnett knows what donors want and how fundraisers can
provide it. *The Zen of Fundraising* illustrates simple yet hard-earned
lessons through which fundraisers can engage their donors as real
partners, raising more money than ever. But to succeed, fundraisers
need to aspire to greater levels of communication and donor
engagement. This books shows us how.'
Chuck Longfield, founder and CEO, Target Software Inc, USA.

'The refreshingly brief principles provide inspiration and learning to
anyone striving for exceptional fundraising practice.'
Nicci Dent, director of fundraising, Médecins sans Frontières, Australia.

'A gentle blend of humour, personal experiences and practical
examples (but underpinned by pure steel), this book makes the
most compelling case yet for thinking about donor relationships.'
Adrian Sargeant, adjunct professor of philanthropy, Indiana University
Center on Philanthropy, USA.

Relationship Fundraising: A Donor-based Approach to the Business of Raising Money (second edition)

by Ken Burnett
Published by Jossey-Bass Inc in association with The White Lion Press Limited. Hardback, 384 pp.
ISBN 0-7879-6089-6

Ken Burnett has completely revised and updated his classic book *Relationship Fundraising*. Filled with illustrative case examples, donor profiles and more than 200 action points, this ground-breaking book shows fundraisers how to:

• Implement creative approaches to relationship-building fundraising.

• Avoid common fundraising errors and pitfalls.

• Apply the vital ingredients for fundraising success.

• Build good relationships with donors through marketing.

• Achieve a greater understanding of donors.

• Communicate effectively with donors – using direct mail, the press, television, the telephone, face-to-face contact, and more.

• Prepare for the challenges of twenty-first century fundraising.

'Not since Harold Seymour's classic, *Designs for Fund Raising*, has a book of this magnitude come along.

'Ken Burnett's updated and expanded work, *Relationship Fundraising*, just may be the book to which fundraising professionals turn for the next several decades.

'It is as brilliant as it is heartfelt, as simple as it is eloquent.'
Jerry Cianciolo, *The Compleat Professional's Library*, *Contributions Magazine*, USA.

'Ken Burnett's observations, insights and practical tips for building and sustaining relationships are superb. Highly readable, this book is a solid mix of sound theory and pragmatic application.'
Kay Sprinkel Grace, author, *Beyond Fund Raising*; co-author *High Impact Philanthropy*, USA.

'This is the book that sets the agenda for fundraising communications in the twenty-first century. Engaging, inspiring, and thought-provoking, *Relationship Fundraising* is based on the unique 25-year experience of one of the world's most respected fundraisers.'

Bernard Ross, director, The Management Centre, UK; co-author, *Breakthrough Thinking for Nonprofit Organizations*.

Friends for Life: Relationship Fundraising in Practice

by Ken Burnett
Hardback, 599 pp.
ISBN 0-9518971-2-8

Amid the widespread acclaim that greeted the 1992 publication of Ken Burnett's *Relationship Fundraising* was one persistent qualified comment. Essentially the question was 'relationship fundraising sounds very attractive, but will it help us raise more money?'

In this accessible and entertaining sequel, Ken Burnett describes how relationship fundraising is working in a wide variety of organisations in the USA, Canada and the United Kingdom. Their stories provide the answer: a loud and resounding 'yes!'

But the ideas and experiences described in this book will do much more than just help fundraisers raise more money. They will show them how to develop and maintain strong, healthy, mutually beneficial relationships with their donors; relationships that will enable them to make friends for life.

The sequel to *Relationship Fundraising* first appeared in 1996, to international acclaim.

'I'm an enthusiastic fan of Ken Burnett's approach to building friends for life. His new book builds on the practical, common-sense approach to donor development he is famous for advocating.

'Great examples, an easy read – I highly recommend *Friends for Life: Relationship Fundraising in Practice.*'
Dr Judith E Nichols, CFRE, author and consultant, USA.

'*Friends for Life* is a witty, readable tour of donor-think from both sides of the Atlantic and brings together a unique collection of experiences and anecdotes from many world-class fundraisers. *Relationship Fundraising* is already a classic throughout the world and this sequel is sure to have a similar impact.'
Jennie Thompson, consultant and co-founder of Craver, Mathews, Smith and Company, USA.

'The Botton Village case history is riveting. Its lessons have a relevance beyond fundraising. This is what direct marketing should always be, but so seldom is.'
Graeme McCorkell, author and consultant, UK.

Asking Properly: The Art of Creative Fundraising

by George Smith
Hardback, 220 pp.
ISBN 0-9518971-1-X

You will never read a book quite like this. George Smith tears open the conventional wisdom of fundraising creativity and so changes the rules for an entire trade. This book is irreverent, funny, savagely critical and genuinely inspiring, often on the same page.

Asking Properly is almost certainly the most authoritative book ever written about the creative aspects of fundraising. It is likely to remain a key text for years to come.

The author offers a profound analysis of donor motivation and is critical of the extent to which charities take their supporters for granted. But this book is no mere commentary on current practice – it offers a comprehensive checklist on how to optimise the creative presentation of the fundraising message. How to write, design, use direct mail, press advertising, broadcast media and the telephone, how to think in terms of fundraising products... the whole gallery of creativity and media is surveyed and assessed, with hundreds of examples of fundraising campaigns from around the world illustrating the need to 'ask properly'.

The book will prove invaluable to anyone involved in the fundraising process. It is provocative, entertaining and, above all, highly instructive. Read it, apply its lessons and it must enable you to raise more money.

'This book will become a classic. It's not just inspirational and a great read, there's a practical benefit on every page. When you apply George Smith's secrets you can hardly fail to improve your fundraising.'
Harvey McKinnon, president, Harvey McKinnon Associates, Canada.

'It's typically George Smith: wise, uncompromising, devastatingly critical of poor fundraising, brilliantly illustrative of what is good, full of ideas, funny, marvellously written – and exceptionally good value. In short, *Asking Properly* is one of those very few books you will keep for life.'
Pierre-Bernard Le Bas, head of fundraising, UNHCR, Switzerland.